THOUGHTS FROM THE SHORE

by

Lyndsey H Greer

Front Cover: Catriona Henderson Darroch – Celtic Horses
www.flickr.com/photos/cowalcat/

For

my daughter

Greer

who makes every day better
than the one before.

“Tension is who you think you should be
Relaxation is who you are.”

Chinese Proverb

Introduction

Taking time out to reflect on yourself, your life, and how you are living can make all the difference to whether or not you succeed in achieving what you want for yourself. Continually living on a hamster wheel - going round and around, never changing, never learning from your mistakes - will get you nowhere. I learned this the hard way years ago and taking time to discover mindfulness, and techniques to de-stress, as well as taking ownership of my choices, helped me to survive.

We all have a story. After all, that's the point of living. To create your own story and leave a legacy from which others can learn.

Your story may take some time to come together. You may feel that you are wandering along in a haze, a fog that never clears. But one day, after learning, growing, changing, gaining clarity of understanding as to who you really are, you will find your own way home. To a place within yourself where you feel comfortable in your own skin, loving and respecting yourself, and in doing so, you will give back to the world in so many positive and wonderful ways.

You don’t need accolades.

You don’t need others respect.

You don’t need others belief.

Learn to love yourself and therefore radiate love.

Learn to respect yourself and therefore radiate respect.

Learn to understand yourself

and therefore radiate understanding.

It is in becoming you that you radiate the best of you.

Autumn

September - October - November

Autumn comes with the thankfulness of the Harvest to the shore. Greens turn to russets and reds, golden and brown – an encore to the summer, the finale before the Winter. Evening Mists start to form, drifting their way down the Loch serenely

When I think of Autumn, I think of eating peas from the pod, raspberries bursting with juice straight from the cane and enjoying an Indian Summer, as we are often blessed with on the West Coast of Scotland, sunny , crisp cool days with the smell of autumnal decay in the air mingled with the wood smoke from the shore cottages.

We reflect on our own Harvest – the good and the bad.

I love autumn for its offering to us after we have enjoyed the summer sun on our faces (and the summer rain to be fair). It's so generous in its bounty and we give grateful thanks. Every year brings blessings and challenges and it is how we use that year, how we deal with the different situations presented before us that builds our characters, and our resilience.

"It's Character Building Lyndsey," my mother used to say when yet another challenge had appeared in my life. "It's not what has happened to us but how we deal with it that counts."

I would often reply, "My character is big enough! I don't want to have to deal with any more."

"God only sends you what he knows you can deal with at any one time." She would say

What does He know I used to think? I had a lot to learn.

Autumn for me is the start of the year. It is the season to reflect and review; to think of the coming year after the Harvest. The seasons of the year are not only for nature but for us as well. We are undoubtedly connected.

In taking time to look back over the past year, we can do our own Harvesting. What has gone well for us? What would you love to happen in the year ahead? What didn't go well and what can we afford to prune from our lives?

The things that have served us well and deserve to stay, travel with us into the next year and those things that are no longer serving us positively, can be pruned.

Recognise yourself – learn self-awareness. We all build coping strategies to deal with situations. Being independently strong can be exhausting but when you've built a brick wall around you, it's easier to keep it intact than to try and take it apart and bring it down. Too scary by far. And yet to really grow into your true potential, becoming vulnerable can be your biggest show of strength yet. So, remove the bricks, one at a time, let the light in and allow yourself to see the sun.

In reflection and using mediation or mindfulness, we can gain perspective. This can help us to understand what we need in our lives to make us feel whole, to shed old patterns of thinking in order to grow and to become the best of ourselves.

If you can appreciate what is good and then focus on how you really want your life to be, set your intentions and put the actions in place to make it happen.

Think of you and your life and reflect on what has been achieved, what has been learnt, and what to change going forward.

A time to lay new plans.

A great time to declutter, both physically and mentally, digitally too in this modern world.

Recognising those things and those people that are truly important to you, and where you want your life to be, ready for the next Harvest.

Build your goals, say to yourself, if I look back in one years' time, what would I have liked to have achieved, where would I like my life to be, what would I like my life to look like … And then plan to make it happen a step at a time.

All around there is change - globally, nationally, locally.

Jobs, lives, challenges – more often we realise that everything we do is connected to one another.

Connection is Key. It's what binds us together. It's how we work with one another, show respect, be thoughtful.

For all of our actions, there is a reaction.

In all that you do, be kind, be aware of the way you act.

Let them be positive actions that ripple outward.

"Whatever affects one directly,
affect all indirectly."

Martin Luther King Jr

Values

How do you value yourself? What values do you reflect upon the world and how do others value you?

Living your values is important. Anytime I have lost sight of my own values and tried to live by the values imposed on me by others (or that I allowed them to impose on me) was a disaster.

Look inward to your heart, are you happy with the values you have set for yourself and how you live them? If you have made mistakes in the past, have you learnt from them? Have you forgiven yourself for them? And have you grown as a person?

It is in learning and growing that we value ourselves more. In being kind to ourselves and to others, we find grace and peace and learn to be comfortable in our own skin.

Live your values, see the best in yourself and let the dark fade away from your life to leave only the light.

Being busy all the time is not constructive in the long term.

If you want to strive forward remember that you can’t drink from an empty cup.

Take time to reenergise, reflect and refocus.

Today take time to rest, give thanks and reflect on the many, many good things there are in your life, before you start renewed tomorrow.

“Consult not your fears but your hopes and dreams.
Think not about your frustrations but about
your unfulfilled potential. Concern yourself not
with what you tried and failed in but with
what is still possible for you to do.”

Pope John Paul XXIII

There are times when we can all feel hurt. Hurt with bereavement, by illness, by unfeeling comments and actions of those who are power-hungry and unfeeling, and sometimes just because our souls are sensitive, and we feel the weight of the world upon us.

In the midst of the hurt, I challenge you to find the light in the darkness.

I had the joy of my four-year old neighbour, a gorgeous girl, who I shall always think of as Pollyanna, rushing out to greet me when I arrived home from a particularly difficult few days. I had been on the road travelling, weather had been hard, work had been stressful and the days long. In her haste to reach me, she didn't see or feel the rain, she ran, face beaming with a glorious smile and threw her arms around me. She reminded me that love and kindness can break down the biggest of barriers.

Never underestimate the power of a hug and knowing that someone wants to share one with you.

"One day someone is going to hug you so tight that all of your broken pieces will stick together."

Unknown

In life, you will not feel supported by everyone. Sometimes even the people who you think or hope would see your worth, don’t.

They find fault in all that you do and are negative about your goals for your life and they put you down.

Learn to respect yourself and rise above the naysayers, those that continually want to bring you down.

Know your worth, your own gifts and talents and be aware of how much you give to the world around you by just being you.

In knowing, this gives you grace, and with Grace there is calm.

“Everything we hear is an opinion, not a fact. Everything we see is a perspective, not the truth.”

Marcus Aurelius

Life can surprise you when you are facing a change – without asking, friends do extraordinary actions to help you, thoughtfulness you never expected from strangers, support on the new path.

Don’t fear the change, embrace the change.

Who is in your tribe? It’s the tiny things and the big things that matter: a message, a phone call, people going over and above to help you, understanding you, knowing that ‘fine’ doesn’t really mean fine, giving you support when they are struggling with so much themselves.

The people of your tribe are the best of people.

Travelling home from a family wedding, I pondered on the words of the sermon from the ceremony. The theme being based around Agape (the Greek meaning the highest form of love).

Giving of yourself unconditionally in all that you do, in your love for your fellow man.

Being thoughtful and kind around your intentions and your actions.

It can be so easy to hold a piece of yourself back because of the hurts of the past but learning to go forward with kindness and love shows more strength of character, more understanding and more wisdom to know that no matter what has occurred, there is still good in the world. Live your life with Agape.

"Let love be without hypocrisy.
Abhor what is evil; cling to what is good."

Romans 12:9

Autumn – Things to Tend to:

Reflect on what is good in your life?

What depletes and drains your energy?

What have you always dreamed of doing?

Why not start now? What's stopping you?

What are excuses? Your barriers?

Start to plan – carefully

Lay down your thoughts

Be patient

Be kind to yourself

Practice Mindfulness

And breathe

Winter

December - January - February

The Winter Gales have started howling straight up the loch, bringing the cold freezing air from the Baltic, encouraging us to 'Coorie in' – a wonderful Scottish phrase for being cosy by the fire in your home with those you love.

'Coorie in' and the storms will pass. A fabulous analogy for life.

Winter for me is about sitting with all your reflections and new ideas from autumn and planning for the year to come. We know what we want to keep in our lives, what has gone well, what we have pruned and what we are letting go – sending it away with love, thanking it for what it brought into our lives and for the learnings we were taught and the accompanied growth.

Now we are planning and looking at what we would like to bring into our lives for the coming year. What have we always wanted in our lives? New friends, community, a new job, a new home, a new relationship, a change of career, to travel, to study; the list is endless and personal to you.

Start with the end in mind. Your next job might give you the experience and learning for the job you really want to aim for in the future.

Ask yourself what energises your soul? Too long my focus was on survival – how did I put food in the table, petrol in the car, clothes on our backs, afford to pay the bills. I was short term goal focused instead of standing back and looking at the long term and how I was going to get there strategically.

Winter provides us with the planning time. Wrapping up warm for a bracing winter walk along the shore or up through the forests, has a marvellous way of providing clarity of mind. Mindfulness Walking – clearing your thoughts and allowing space for noticing the sky, the sea, the calling of the sea birds, the wind on your face – how does everything look, feel, taste, sound and smell. Using our senses and coming back into line with nature can really help us to think clearly.

The new ideas come filtering in, you remember who you truly are, what you always wanted to do, to be.

Winter can be harsh on the shore - strong winds with relentless rain hitting you horizontally and you wonder if the storm will ever pass. We don't suffer many frosts here being so close to the sea but we have the benefit of being able to look towards the mountains of Loch Lomond, the Arrochar Alps and further south to the towering sleeping giants of Arran.

Perspective - how easy it can be to let the little things trouble you. A sinful waste of energy and allowing yourself to be bullied by … you!!

The storms do pass and sometimes without really realising, through the storm, whilst we are 'coorieing in', having felt bashed around by the world, we are growing, healing and learning.

You can't go through a storm and come out of the other side the same person as you were before. You have changed, you have learned something new, and your perspective has shifted.

You can decide whether to remain bitter about the whole experience and waste your life in negativity or you can decide to understand the lesson, your growth, and use it for your future good and the good of others.

Let it go and move forward.

Easier said than done, I know, but far better for you, your life and for your relationships.

Allow winters gifts to do just this for your soul. Walk in the wind, embrace the cold, delight in the returning sun as the days slowly lengthen. Use the time to plan, to work constructively on yourself, to allow yourself to understand the different perspectives of the situation you found yourself in and allow yourself to breathe and shed a skin, a layer of bricks on that wall you have been building around yourself so carefully.

Protection is one thing but when it keeps out the sun, it is a cold and lonely place.

When I visited Iceland and Norway, I adored the custom of keeping a candle lit at all times. The lands of the north are so many hours in darkness through the winter,that tradition calls for candlelight to be burning at all times, a promise of warmer days and the return of the sun. A symbol of hope. Something I love to do throughout the winter in my own home, is to have a candle burning, bringing in hope, giving continual light.

The first Sunday in advent at Christmas represents Hope so keep a light burning through the Winter and beyond, both within your heart and in your home to remind you that no matter how harsh the storm or how long it lasts, it will pass and the light will always be there guiding you to the start of spring and a new hope.

"Hope is being able to see light despite all the darkness."

Desmond Tutu

The Second Sunday in Advent is about Peace. Very apt considering the world we live in today with heightened terrorism threats, knife crime and political turmoil.

But peace comes from our own inner peace first. Coming to terms with 'our lot' where we are in life, our challenges, our blessings, the choices we have made and making the most of who we are for ourselves and for others.

Being peaceful is a mindset. Others may not agree with your choices, you may not agree with theirs. Understanding one another better and accepting our differences goes a long way to a peaceful existence. Be calm and peaceful in the stressful run up to Christmas.

"Do not let the behaviour of others
destroy your inner peace."
Dalai Lama

The third Sunday in Advent (also known as Gaudete Sunday) represents Joy.

How do we define Joy? A moment of laughter, time spent with friends, a smile, a hug, music that touches your soul, a beautiful scene?

I've always found that thinking of something joyful or something that has brought me joy, lifts the moment.

Joy brings light.

Find your joy in the smallest of moments, it brings you comfort. Find your joy and share it with others, everyone is walking a difficult path.

"Find out where joy resides and give it a voice far beyond singing. For to miss the joy is to miss all."

Robert Louis Stevenson

The fourth Sunday in Advent represents Love. Preparation for Christmas brings me great joy.

Home cooking, favourite recipes, local produce and organic vegetables from the garden, homemade mince pies, blackcurrant jam, spiced apple chutney and mums curry dip (it wouldn't be Christmas without it).

I love bringing the traditions of the past together with new traditions that we started in our new home by the sea.

Putting love into all that we do and taking the time to enjoy it with all of your senses, heightens the moment, bringing memories of those who have gone and not forgotten, together with creating new memories with those who are with us now.

When we head into a new year, consider your focus for this year and beyond.

I remember at School we wrote a note on where we wanted to be by the year 2032 - the year we would all reach 65 and in theory retire. It seemed so far away then, eons ahead and now it feels so close.

So what to do to make every moment count, every memory last? Understand our purpose for doing anything and then focus.

Too many years I have been distracted, putting off what I desired, feeling the weight of responsibility that came first.

Formulate your plan and include plans B and C – it's good to be flexible. Allow room for surprises, learn to go with the flow, be available for new ideas and opportunities.

What are your plans for the year? They don't need to be big or fancy, they just need to be yours.

Let’s talk about energisers and detractors.

Energisers - those things you love to do and people in your life that increase your energy, refill your soul and build you up.

Detractors - those things you dislike and people in your life that drain your energy and leave you empty.

Take a moment to understand what energises you and fills your soul. Life is too short for the detractors - don’t give them your energy.

We sometimes don’t realise that we are pushing ourselves hard, trying to be all things to all people, get through the To Do list which , to be fair, seems never ending.

Demands will always be on us and self-care has to be the priority. What use will any of us be to anyone else, if first we don’t fill our own batteries?

I’ve read and watched a few books and videos on the subject, ‘self-care starts in the kitchen,’ and ‘self-care starts with exercise,’ but quite frankly and simply - self-care starts with you.

The winter months are about hibernation, getting ready for the coming spring. Plant your seeds of ideas to ensure that come spring, you will be ready to enjoy the new growth.

“You, yourself , as much as anybody in the entire universe, deserve your love and affection.”

Buddha

After a break in the weather where blue skies were seen for a couple of hours, I awoke one morning to the rain and wind on my window. I reminded myself it was the depths of Winter and at least the weather was seasonal.

I have started longing for the spring, those mornings when you wake up and there is a slight change in the air and a feeling of hope as the light becomes stronger. But then I catch myself. Wishing for something that can't happen right now only makes us unhappy and we don't embrace the present.

Days by the fire, the spring bulbs pushing through the ground, time to be inside and hibernate a little.

Learn to live in the moment, not to relive the past in your mind or constantly wait for the future - just enjoy today.

It's a far more peaceful way of being.

Enjoy the moment - it is fleeting.

"And as the snow falls in the river,
a moment white, then gone forever."

Robert Burns, Tam O'Shanter

At times when we know we could have acted in a better way; for instance when we are disappointed in not being appreciated for something and we go into a mood; when we think others are judging us, rather than supporting us; when we have genuinely praised and lifted others up and they have seen it as insincere.

So wrong. Since when has being sincere been so misconstrued. We are so used to others bringing us down that we miss the glitter amongst the rubbish.

Genuine can appear in the form of family calling to check in, a best friend dropping by and making you laugh, friends who go out of their way to do something special, messages from caring pals and neighbours and friends with their kindness and help just when you need it.

The nuggets of genuine friendship, of those who lift you up, who know you and accept you for you.

Don't let the negativity find you, find the genuine and focus on it, believe and know that you are loved.

It's one of the greatest gifts you can give yourself, to forgive. Forgive everybody."

Maya Angelou

Bereavement

At times my mind turns to memories. We lost my amazing father over 30 years ago and he was joined in heaven by my mum 28 years later.

My childhood was filled with uncomplicated carefree days. No responsibility, gifts of education, horse riding, music lessons, holidays and family time. If only I had realised then how blessed I was.

I could spend time grieving for what I have lost and the learns I have taken from the difficult moments but I find it cathartic to remember the laughter.

It's in the good memories we find solace, the gratefulness for having known those times, a realisation that to live the legacy is an honour - I still see him now in the tenacity towards work of his granddaughter, in her eyes and in her laughter. Our loved ones live on in us and in our work and play. They are with us always in more ways than we may ever see.

Remember the good times with your passed loved ones and be grateful for all the new memories you are making in the present.

Live in the moment and look forward to all the great times still to come.

So much change at once.

The old passing into new.

But memories don't fade, keep them close to your heart and laugh often as you remember the good times, the family times and the close times.

"The secret of change is to focus all of your energy, not on fighting the old but on building the new."

Socrates

Winter: Things to Tend to:

Nurture Yourself

Eat Healthily

Sleep – find ways to help you relax

Make small step changes, make them strong before taking the next step

Bring more of what you love into your life

Respect Yourself

Practice gratefulness

Practise mindfulness

Rest

Smile

Spring

March - April - May

And breathe, spring is here. Rejoice, I love the reminders of spring throughout the winter - in the arrival of snowdrops in late January/early February, daffodils and crocus in March – a glimpse of what is to come.

Slowly but surely the gales die down , the days lengthen and the sun starts to reach into my courtyard garden, which for months has lain in wait for the sun to be high enough in the sky so that the rays can land on the raised beds and warm the earth, encouraging new growth.

I love to walk through the woods in spring, watching the bluebells pushing through, hearing the cuckoo down the glen and I wonder whose home he is wrecking today. A devious and strategic bird, a lesson for us all in life to watch out!

At the allotment, the earth is warming up and pleasure lies in planting kale, beetroot, potatoes, peas, beans, and carrots. The allotment provides me with so many surprises and delights, watching the plants grow – their main focus in life – just to get on and grow and produce a fabulous harvest in the autumn.

No distractions, no waste of energy worrying about other things – but to just grow.

Aligning yourself with nature and the seasons is very rewarding. Spring expands your ideas, those seeds of thoughts you had, slowly taking root, growing bigger and stronger with every day.

Be gentle with your plans and new growth at this time, you have just come through autumn and winter - it hasn't necessarily been an easy ride and now you are setting out into a fresh new world. Take your time, take your lessons with you but not the walls.

Allow the sun in, to reach your roots, your soul, and your heart. A day at a time, a moment at a time.

Then slowly but surely you build in strength. Take any knock backs with measure, review, refocus and then go again the next day.

Life is resilience. Life is perseverance. Life is strength and in all of this, it's about finding the sun in the rain. Laughing in the face of adversity and shouting 'Bring it On!'

Rest when you need but never give up. The road to recovery can be two steps forward and three steps back, but as long as you keep moving forward, all is good. Set your own pace, this is not a competition.

You think that another person is doing well, that they are way ahead of you, at a different stage. You ask yourself, why am I not at that stage? Why am I not doing better?

Focus on your own path, don't be distracted. I am a great believer that everyone is at the right place on their path, right here, right now. You might not agree but the sooner you accept it, the quicker you will move along it.

Live your life with purpose and direction and revel in the lessons you learn along the way, the people you meet and the laughs you share.

"Comparison is the thief of all joy."

Theodore Roosevelt

Happiness

What does happiness really mean?

I think it means so many different things - receiving a hug, a beautiful smile, being told that you are loved, watching a beloved child blossom and grow , following your purpose in life, being in the flow.

For me it is a sense of contentment, when at long last, after a painful journey inward, you truly find yourself, forgiving those who hurt you and forgiving yourself.

Enjoy being truly you and being in the flow.

“Happiness is when what you think,
what you say and what you do are in harmony.”
Mahatma Gandhi

Look back at your life, the path that lies out behind you. You can see the times of hardship, of difficulties and of delight and pleasure.

We don't celebrate enough about how much we persevered, kept going, drove on, even when we wanted to pull the duvet over our head and say, "Not today thank you."

Never underestimate the hero inside yourself. Celebrate it, applaud it and give it the biggest pat on the back and put on your cape.

You are truly amazing.

Friendship

Friendships come in many forms - those you have known for years, new friends not long met, colleagues who step up and have your back, friends who have been in your life and for many different reasons, or are no longer a part of it.

Such a blessing when you come together with people you haven't seen for many years and it feels like it could be yesterday, the friends that you have mis-understandings with but with whom you can have an adult conversation and you sort out your differences, growing stronger for the lesson

Those that love you just as you are, appreciate you for all your gifts and understand your flaws are always there for you. Repair your flaws with gold – just like "kintsukuroi"

Fill your life with friends who love and appreciate the wonderful you - just as you are.

"A sweet friendship refreshes the soul."
Proverbs 27:9

Perception

Each of us has a different perception of events - how we feel, think, judge, or don't judge, about situations, people and our own lives.

There is a saying that if you haven't walked a mile in someone else's shoes, then you cannot understand how they feel from their perspective. In other words, learn to practice empathy.

See life from a different perspective and judge less.

"Do not conform to the pattern of this world,
but be transformed by the renewing of your mind."

Romans 12.2

Choices

Many times in our lives we make a choice.

If we have listened to our intuition, the choice we make should enhance the person we are, letting our light shine.

If we take a choice outside of our intuition, you find yourself on a path that does not resonate with your soul.

We become less than we could have been, we dull our sparkle - the light leaves our souls.

Make choices wisely that are guided by your intuition, that are good for you and let your light shine so brightly, you dazzle others.

Be not afraid of being fabulous.

"Shine like the whole universe is yours."

Rumi

On the first Mother's Day after my mum had passed, I remember times over the last few years. I had fallen into the habit, on my daily visits, of opening the front door and shouting "Hello", a wee shout of "Hello," would come back and then, "It's good to see your face."

When my daughter was three, I had the opportunity to travel with work to Jordan for five days. She stayed with her Nan and Grandad and when I came home, my daughter was so relieved to see me, she took my face, a hand on each cheek, holding it still and starred and starred into my eyes, delighted to see me.

Go out into the world and smile at the faces, they will smile back. Share your gifts and connect with your loved ones. The physical presence of seeing each other is worth gold.

"Children are the anchors that hold a mother to life."

Sophocles

When something difficult or distressing happens in our lives, we sometimes only see the negative aspects of the situation. But so very often, a positive comes out of the moment that would not have happened without the lesson of the challenge we had grown through.

See the rainbow after the rain or at least the hope of a rainbow if the rain is still falling.

"Barns burnt down ... now I can see the Moon."

Masahide

Judgement

You cannot understand that person's journey through judging them by their looks, clothes and what others have said about them.

You cannot understand another person by judging them at all.

Take time to peel the layers back and see the gifts that lie below the surface of everyone.

We are all connected, all walking our own paths - it's easier to walk your path if there are people along the way supporting and encouraging, rather than condemning.

See the light of love in everyone you meet and everywhere you go.

Be kind to each other and be kind to yourself.

Remember to take time to relax and reflect and say Thank you.
Remember to take time out of your busy day to just Be.

A calm mind is an effective mind.

"Have regular hours for work and play; make each day both useful and pleasant, and prove that you understand the worth of time by employing it as well."

Louisa May Alcott

Spring: Things to Tend to:

Turn your face into the sun and embrace the warmth

Be grateful for all that you have in your life

Find the positive in everything

Congratulate yourself for all the positive steps you have made

Take bricks down from your outer wall
– one at a time- very slowly but surely

Take any knockbacks in proportion.

Acknowledge them, take stock and move forward again

Be kind to yourself

Practice Mindfulness

Nurture Yourself

Smile

Summer

June - July - August

The sunlight is dazzling out on the loch, the sailing boats drift by, caught by the gentle breeze and summer bathes us all in her warm embrace.

If we are lucky, the ‘Waverley’ may sail past, reminding us of the heydays of the paddle steamers on the Clyde plying their trade between Argyll, the Isles and Glasgow.

I love to sit and watch the summer sunrise, coming up over the hills to the East, over the waters of the Loch, the most beautiful time of day. The silence, nothing stirs, perhaps just a gentle ripple from the ferries across the way, starting their day.

An oystercatcher flies by followed by a cormorant. A silent winged heron makes her way to fish in the shallows and the day begins.

Summer is growing season. You’ve made your reflections in the autumn, planted your seeds, they have lain dormant through the winter, ready for the spring and fresh shoots of growth.

You have tended them well, cared for the seeds of your dreams and of your goals. You have watered them, fed them, nurtured them and given them every chance of life.

Now it's time to grow. All that hard work is at long last coming into its own, becoming reality. You've worked for this and don't stop now. Keep the focus, keep tending to your dreams.

Feed, water and cultivate them – without focus and intention, your ideas could wither or run in different directions than you weren't expecting or wanting,

Time to prune and pull in the straggling ideas brings us to autumn again and the cycle of the year completes.

Let ideas mature, seeds from that maturity, will take root and grow into the new – emergent, and divergent, strategies – remember to keep the focus on maintaining your foundations too.

Strong foundations are the basis for all that you do in life. Nurture yourself, forgive yourself if you get it wrong, nurture your relationships, forgive others if they make mistakes, nurture your beliefs, nurture your dreams. Learn to just 'Be you'.

Too many times I feel people think of themselves as fighting battles alone, that no one else feels the way that they do, and that independence is the only way to deal with a problem.

It’s the positive relationships in your life that hold you up, support and understand you. Those who take the time to encourage you, make the difference. And in return receive mutual encouragement.

Take the time to encourage and uplift one another.

Love is all there is, life is too short. Be kind out there.

Life’s true gift lies in your freedom to design it beautifully. With each rise of the sun, you get to chase the opportunity to fill your days with meaning—to live your life the way you choose.

How lucky we are and how grateful I am

Communication

How often do you find you are miles away in your thinking compared to that of someone else?

Perceptions are distorted when we don't know the whole picture

Don't make assumptions, try to understand and realise that we need to be non-judgemental.

Think before acting

Be kind and be understanding - the world is a tough place these days, we need one another.

Transition and Transformation

I believe that sometimes we put too much pressure on ourselves to be all things to all people. That we think we can take on the world and do it alone. But change takes time and being comfortable with that change takes even longer.

We forget how much there is to learn, to do and to embrace. If we try to do it all, we just fail in all areas instead of excelling in any.

That is why planning goals carefully and with long-sightedness is so important. We talk about being kind to ourselves, but I think we forget what that really means.

Set your goals reasonably, step by step, give time for development, speak kindly but with honesty to yourself and remember to take time to celebrate when the goals are achieved. Slowly, progressively you will build yourself a strong foundation from which to fly.

Connectedness

We are all in some way connected to one another. Our interactions, feelings and thoughts create our life.

What we believe we are, we will be.

Being connected to one another or reconnecting can be cathartic. We support, encourage and laugh together to support one another.

Give thanks to all those you are connected too, for their gift of friendship to their sharing of knowledge, insight and laughter.

Take time to see how you are connected to others and be grateful for their presence.

“Whatever affects one directly, affects all indirectly.”

Martin Luther King Jr

Flow

There is a saying in life about being in the flow. When what you do, say and think are all in balance, when life flows with effortless ease. What you desire comes to you without stress, hard work or angst.

I love being in the flow - you find you are living your life's purpose, loving what you do and giving to others all at the same time.

Find your flow and let it take you in the direction you love.

"Happiness is when what you think,
what you say and what you do are in harmony."

Mahatma Gandhi

Giving of yourself completely, unconditionally with love can be difficult. When you have been hurt and bruised by the world, we tend to shut down, become hostile and retreat.

Take time to recover, to heal, to regenerate.

Radiate kindness from yourself.

It is in giving of ourselves to others that we gain most joy.

The world is a better place when we are there for each other.

Don’t exclude, include. Don’t judge, understand.

Don’t condemn; show love.

Be your own best friend and that way you will be a best friend to others. Share friendship that is unconditional and excepting, be there for one another, it’s a tough road if you try to walk it alone.

“Pearls don’t lie on the seashore,
if you want one you must dive for it.”

Chinese Proverb

My life has been peppered with a lovely mix - of work with valued clients, meeting new and old friends, making time to relax and meditate, to exercise and socialise.

Balance in our life isn't produced by outside influences, it is created by ourselves - taking charge of our goals and what we want in order to make our life meaningful - being the best of us and supporting and loving others.

Summer Things to Tend to:

Go outside and play

Have a picnic

Give thanks for all that you are achieving

Appreciate each step change and say Well Done

***Nurture your plans, feed them,
keep them strong, prune if necessary***

This isn't a race – everyone is going at their own speed

Respect yourself and your values

Be patient

Be kind to yourself

Practice mindfulness

Smile

Epilogue

Life is about balance.

Balance brings us joy.

*So true. Bringing balance into everything we do,
gives us more joy to every single part of our life.*

Rest so that you can restore your energy.

Laugh so that you can share in a moment.

*Work at your passion so that you may enjoy life
and give back with love.*

Love so that you may love your life.

Share so that you may give of your life to others.

Play so that you give yourself energy.

*Sleep so that you can share the joy of
another day with those you love.*

Be kind to yourself and live your best life.

“Let yourself be silently drawn
by the stronger pull of what you really love.”

- Rumi